GROWING GARDENS

Indoor Gardens

BY EMILY HECK

Kids Core

An Imprint of Abdo Publishing

abdobooks.com

abdobooks.com

Printed in the United States of America, North Mankato, Minnesota.
052025
092025

Cover Photo: Shutterstock Images
Interior Photos: ArtMarie/E+/Getty Images, 4–5; Ashley-Belle Burns/Shutterstock Images, 6; Shutterstock Images, 9, 10, 12–13, 14, 17, 18, 23, 26, 28 (bottom), 29 (top); ozgurcankaya/E+/Getty Images, 20–21; Olya Haifisch/Shutterstock Images, 24; Scisetti Alfio/Shutterstock Images, 28 (top); iStockphoto, 29 (bottom)

Editor: Christa Kelly
Series Designer: Katharine Hale

Library of Congress Control Number: 2024948989

Publisher's Cataloging-in-Publication Data

Names: Heck, Emily, author.
Title: Indoor gardens / by Emily Heck
Description: Minneapolis, Minnesota: Abdo Publishing, 2026 | Series: Growing gardens | Includes online resources and index.
Identifiers: ISBN 9781098297411 (lib. bdg.) | ISBN 9798384919933 (ebook)
Subjects: LCSH: Gardens--Juvenile literature. | Gardening--Juvenile literature. | Indoor gardens--Juvenile literature. | Horticulture--Juvenile literature.
Classification: DDC 635.3--dc23

CONTENTS

Many stores sell tropical plants year-round.

Thriving Inside

Levi and his dad were shopping at a plant store. A plant with big green leaves caught Levi's eye. The tag said it was called a gardenia. Levi and his dad bought the plant and brought it home. They put it in a dim corner in their living room.

Gardeners should check their plants often for signs of illness, such as yellow leaves.

After a few weeks, the plant's leaves started turning yellow. Levi was worried. He was watering the plant. He gave it **fertilizer**. What could be wrong?

Levi's dad took him to the library. They found a book about caring for plants. The book said gardenias need lots of sunlight. Levi and his dad moved the plant near a big window.

Levi watched the plant anxiously. At first, nothing changed. But after a few weeks, the leaves turned green. Then the gardenia made a flower! The plant was healthy again.

On Levi's birthday, his dad bought him another plant. Levi put it next to the gardenia. He looked at the plants proudly. He loved taking care of his indoor garden.

Growing Indoors

Indoor gardens are good options for people who don't have yards or outdoor areas.

Indoor gardens don't require much space. People can place potted plants throughout their homes. Potted plants can go on shelves or tables. They can even hang from ceilings.

Plants can help decorate a space. They add shapes and textures to a room. They also add color. Some even smell nice.

Indoor gardens are also a way for people to have living plants all year. People who live in cold **climates** cannot garden outside during the winter. But plants can still grow indoors.

What's a Solarium?

A solarium is a room attached to a house where plants can grow. The walls and ceiling are made of glass. This lets in plenty of light. Solariums are great places for indoor gardens.

Gardening is a great way to learn about nature.

Growing plants indoors lets people enjoy nature from their homes.

Plants have many benefits. They make **oxygen** for people to breathe. Some studies show that plants can even clean the air.

Indoor gardens also help people feel happy and calm. Some plants are especially good at improving moods. For example, palm plants might remind people of a tropical beach. This can help people feel relaxed. Having an indoor garden is a great way to bring nature inside.

Primary Source

Mengmeng Gu is a professor. She teaches people about plants. She says:

> Different **properties** of plants, such as how they look, smell, and feel, impact us in so many ways. They can feel good to the touch, make a space more fragrant, and please our eyes.

Source: Lala Tanmoy Das. "What Science Tells Us about the Mood-Boosting Effects of Indoor Plants," *Washington Post*, 7 June 2022, washingtonpost.com. Accessed 5 Sept. 2024.

Comparing Texts

Does this quote support the information in this chapter? Or does it give a different perspective? Explain how in a few sentences.

Even young children can grow plants indoors.

CHAPTER 2

Planning an Indoor Garden

Houses and apartments are full of places to put plants. People keep plants in kitchens, home offices, bathrooms, and bedrooms. But different plants have different needs. Certain plants grow better in some rooms than others.

Each hibiscus flower generally blooms for only a single day.

Different plants need different amounts of heat and moisture. Tropical plants do well in warm and **humid** spaces, such as bathrooms. Desert plants do best in dry areas. A sunny living room might be a good place to keep a desert plant.

Different plants also need different amounts of light. Some plants need a lot of light. Hibiscuses need at least six hours of sunlight each day. They should be placed near windows.

Artificial Light

Sunlight is best for plants. But **artificial** light can help too. People can buy special grow lights for their plants. These lights give the plant energy. Artificial light can make up for the lack of sunlight in a space.

When choosing a spot for an indoor garden, people must keep plants away from pets. Many indoor plants are **toxic** to cats and dogs. Chinese evergreen and English ivy plants can both harm pets.

Popular Indoor Plants

Some indoor plants are very easy to care for. These are best for people who are new to indoor gardening. One example is a snake plant. Snake plants need water only once a month. A ZZ plant is another great plant for beginners. ZZ plants can grow in low light.

Many indoor plants come from tropical climates, such as jungles or rainforests. These plants are used to warm temperatures.

ZZ plants are also known as Zanzibar gems.

Many grow in shady spots in nature. This makes them good houseplants. Prayer plants and peace lilies are tropical plants that are often grown indoors. Orchids and African violets are also popular tropical indoor plants.

Some people grow succulents in glass containers called terrariums.

Desert plants are common houseplants too. Many of these plants are succulents. Succulents store water inside their leaves. Aloe vera and jade plants are succulents. Cacti are also succulents. They have prickly spines. These types of plants can be good additions to an indoor garden.

Further Evidence

Look at the website below. Does it give any new evidence to support Chapter Two?

Succulents

abdocorelibrary.com/indoor-gardens

Most plants grow best in containers a little larger than the plants.

CHAPTER 3

Growing an Indoor Garden

It's important to have the right supplies for an indoor garden. Gardeners should start by choosing containers in which to grow their plants. The containers should have drainage holes in the bottom. This allows extra water to drain from the soil.

A tray underneath the container can catch the water.

Next, gardeners should choose their soil. Most indoor plants grow best in regular potting soil. But some plants need other types of soil. Succulents grow best in sandy soil. People can buy premade succulent soil at garden stores.

Decorating the Space

Once the plants are potted, gardeners can put the plants in their new spots. Plants can go almost anywhere. Bigger pots can go directly on the floor. Smaller pots can go on tables or counters. Plants that like lots of sun can go on windowsills. Plants that like shade can go in corners.

Before bringing a new plant home, people should know where they want to put it. This makes sure people have the right amount of space and sunlight for the new plant.

Some potted plants grow well in plant hangers. Plant hangers let people attach pots to the ceiling. This allows plants with long leaves or vines to grow without taking up too much room. Shelves and wall-mounted planters also help plants take up less room.

Repotting Plants

When plants get too big for their pots, they must be placed in new containers. This is called repotting.

Indoor Garden Care

Indoor plants need regular care. They must be watered on a schedule. But not all plants need the same amount of water. To decide if a plant needs to be watered, gardeners can put a finger into the soil. If the soil is dry under the surface, the plant should be watered. Gardeners should water the base of the plant, not the leaves or flowers. Watering the base sends the water straight to the roots.

Sick Plants

Plants get sick if they are not cared for correctly. Many plants show signs of illness on their leaves. If a plant's leaves are yellow, the plant may have gotten too much water or too little sun. If the tips of the leaves are brown, the plant may be too dry or too cold. Plants without leaves show different signs of illness. Cacti may turn brown or mushy.

Adults can help kids learn to care for plants.

Some plants need to be regularly pruned. Pruning involves cutting away dead leaves or stems. Gardeners can use a pair of scissors or shears to prune plants. Flowering plants should not be pruned until after the flowers have finished blooming. This keeps the plant looking its best. Kids should always get an adult to help them prune plants.

Caring for an indoor garden takes time and work. But it can be a fun hobby. Indoor plants bring joy and beauty into people's homes. And it is rewarding to help the plants grow.

Explore Online

Look at the website below. Does it give any new evidence to support Chapter Three?

Houseplant

abdocorelibrary.com/indoor-gardens

Garden Plants

Spider plant

Spider plants have long, thin leaves. The leaves are green and may have white stripes.

Pothos

Pothos have fast-growing vines with heart-shaped leaves. The leaves are green and can have patches of yellow or white.

String of pearls

String of pearls are succulents. They have pea-shaped leaves that grow on vines.

African violet

African violets have purple, blue, or white flowers and green leaves. The flowers bloom year-round.

Glossary

artificial
describing something made by humans instead of occurring in nature

climates
areas with specific weather patterns

fertilizer
a substance that is added to soil to help plants grow

humid
describing air that has a lot of moisture

oxygen
a gas that is part of the air that people and animals breathe

properties
the traits that make up something

toxic
able to make a living thing sick

Online Resources

To learn more about indoor gardens, visit our free resource websites below.

Visit **abdocorelibrary.com** or scan this QR code for free Common Core resources for teachers and students, including vetted activities, multimedia, and booklinks, for deeper subject comprehension.

Visit **abdobooklinks.com** or scan this QR code for free additional online weblinks for further learning. These links are routinely monitored and updated to provide the most current information available.

Learn More

Allen, Beatrice Boggs and Belle Boggs. *Plant Pets: 27 Cool Houseplants to Grow and Love*. Storey, 2024.

Asseray, Philippe. *My First Indoor Garden*. Skyhorse, 2021.

Murray, Julie. *Plants of the Rain Forest*. Abdo, 2023.

Index

About the Author

Emily Heck is a freelance writer and editor in Minnesota. When she's not writing, she enjoys reading, crafting, and spending time outdoors.